# The Hid of the Game
## Law of Attraction

Version I – 2024

Written by
**ALEX WHITE**

Copyright © 2024
Published by: HUASKA PUBLISHER

*Huaska*
PUBLISHER

# The Hidden Laws of the Game
## Law of Attraction

**Copyright © 2024 | HUASKA PUBLISHER**

All rights reserved. The copying, transcription, reproduction, or use of any part of this work, whether by electronic means or any other existing methods, is strictly prohibited without the proper written authorization from the publishers. Any violation of copyright will be subject to legal consequences.

Both the author and the publisher disclaim responsibility for any potential damages arising from any theory or assumption presented throughout this work. It is the reader's sole responsibility, in their sound mental faculties, to judge whether they will apply any method described in this material. If you choose to implement any suggested procedure, you assume all potential risks and completely absolve the author of any responsibility, as the entire content of this work is considered mere guidance for the current subject.

All the content presented here is purely informative and represents only the personal opinion of the author, without any claim to possess a scientific nature.

**ALL RIGHTS RESERVED BY HUASKA PUBLISHER**

**AUTHOR'S NOTE #1:**

ALEX WHITE is not my real name. It is a pseudonym used to avoid exposing my private life, especially that of my family members. My true name and the names of other individuals in my family will be preserved throughout this work to ensure integrity and privacy.

# PREFACE

Welcome to a journey that unveils the invisible framework governing our lives. We often walk through life feeling as if we're at the mercy of forces beyond our control. But what if there were hidden laws at play—laws that, once understood, could unlock a path to personal power, fulfillment, and true success? This book invites you to view life as a grand game, governed by ancient and universal principles that, when harnessed, can guide us toward our highest aspirations.

The Hidden Laws of the Game reveals essential truths that remain unknown to many yet accessible to all. Each chapter will take you deeper into the foundational laws that shape our world, from vibration and attraction to balance and persistence. These principles are not only timeless but are also deeply woven into the fabric of the universe. Learning to apply them will change the way you think, feel, and act.

As you embark on this exploration, be prepared for a shift in perspective. You may begin to see yourself not merely as a player but as a co-creator in this game of life. By aligning with these hidden laws, you'll gain the tools to manifest your dreams, transcend challenges, and shape your destiny with intention and clarity.

With an open mind and a receptive heart, you will soon understand the wisdom behind the invisible laws that govern us all. I invite you to turn the page and discover the extraordinary journey that awaits.

**ALEX WHITE**

# INTRODUCTION:
## Discovering the Invisible Game

# BEHIND THE CURTAIN

Life is a mystery that unravels in front of our very eyes, full of challenges, opportunities, and moments of complete surprise.

Great minds throughout history have tried to understand the main laws ruling the universe. Nowadays, we are conscious that life is not the result of coincidence; it is a very complicated game of energies, intentions, and actions.

This book will disclose exactly how these invisible forces work and will give you the tools to play this game more consciously and with intention.

## LIFE AS A GAME

Ever think that your life could be paralleled to a game? A game operates on rules, strategies, and objectives. Once we learn the rules of the game, we can then play it masterfully; thus, we make wiser decisions toward the achievement of objectives.

In life, the "rules" come in the way of universal laws: unseen laws which shape our reality and influence the result of our thoughts, actions, and emotions. Without any knowledge about these laws, we do not know the rules of the game and feel lost or frustrated many times.

In the following chapters, we will discover these laws so you may understand how they work and apply them in your favor. Mastering these laws will automatically stop making you an observer, and you will become a player who will not only participate in the play of life but create a path and destiny for your-self.

## THE INVISIBLE LAWS: A HIDDEN REALITY

These are laws that are invisible; however, their manifestations are well seen in every moment of our lives. Reflect on the physical laws: You cannot see gravity, but you can feel its effects.

The same thing occurs with universal laws, which operate at a much more subtle level and dictate the flow of energy manifesting experiences. They interact with our thoughts, feelings, and intentions, assessing what we manifest into our lives, repel, or build upon along our path.

Now, why are these laws invisible? Because they operate at deep levels of consciousness and energy. They can't be seen with the physical eyes but are perceived by those who seek to understand the forces behind appearances. This book will teach you to perceive beyond the obvious-to recognize signs and patterns of these laws in your life.

## THE POWER OF CONSCIOUSNESS AND INTENTION

One of the main secrets of the game of life is the power of your consciousness. The way you think and feel is not just a response to the world but an active force that shapes your reality. By learning to direct your thoughts, intentions, and emotions in alignment with universal laws, you create a powerful vibration that attracts what you desire. This book is, therefore, a guide to awakening consciousness and developing clear intention, allowing you to access the potential in every moment and transform your experience.

The secret to mastering the invisible game is to have clarity about what you want, cultivate an abundance mindset, and act in alignment with your highest intentions. Through this process, you'll realize that your life isn't merely the result of external factors but also a reflection of your inner energy and beliefs.

## THE ROADMAP OF THE JOURNEY

Each chapter in this book will take you another step on a voyage of self-discovery and conscious manifestation. We are going to explore laws such as the Law of Vibration, which explains that through our thoughts and feelings, we create frequencies that connect with similar energies. Also, the Law of Attraction and Repulsion will be explored to show just how we attract what we are and repel what incongruously vibrates at a different frequency from our own. We will also come to understand the Law of Detachment, showing how it is necessary to trust in the flow of life rather than fixate on particular outcomes. Besides those, we have the Law of Inspired Action, which invites us to act upon our inner urges, while the Law of Persistence and Faith will help us stay confident even if results are far away from showing.

## READY TO START THE GAME?

This book is an invitation to a new way of living. By the end of this journey, you will see that life is indeed a grand game where you are both the player and the creator.

What you will discover here is a practical and philosophical guide that will allow you to transform uncertainty into clarity, fear into confidence, and doubt into purpose.

Are you ready to discover the invisible game and begin playing with consciousness and intention? Open your heart and mind to the teachings to come, and allow yourself to explore the infinite potential within you. It's time to learn the rules, take control, and create a reality aligned with your true self.

# CHAPTER I:
## The Law of Vibration

# WHAT IS YOUR EMOTION?

Everything that exists, from most solid to most ethereal-from what is tangible to what is intangible-is fostered by one force in essence: vibration. The Law of Vibration simply says that nothing is ever static. In other words, everything is energy in constant motion, and it manifests in different vibrational frequencies. This not only refers to the objects and matter but also our thoughts, feelings, beliefs, and intentions. That is, your thoughts and feelings have a real, live vibration operating within your reality in ways you don't yet fully understand.

For many, such a statement may be considered bold, perhaps even controversial. After all, we have been programmed to think that reality consists only of that which can be seen and touched. Or does it? If we were to stop and reflect, we'd note that such unseen forces envelop us, inform our lives, and even guide our decisions. Imagine the tension in a room following an argument or the lightness and joy from shared laughter. We can feel those vibrations, even though they are unseen. And those vibrations not only create our experiences but go on to attract circumstances, people, and events that are resonating at the same frequency.

## REALITY IS SHAPED BY YOUR FREQUENCY

If we take on the belief that everything is energy, then everything we want—a new opportunity, healthy relationships, financial success, or personal growth—is also energy. And in order for these things to come into our life, we need to be on the same vibrational frequency that they are on. This is the core of the Law of

Vibration: you attract what vibrates to the same frequency as you. It's simple, yet challenging, because it does call for us to take ownership of our frequency. No excuses; you gotta become what you want so you may attract what you want.

This is probably one of the more 'uncomfortable' yet transformative areas of the Law of Vibration. By saying you are responsible for what you attract into your life, the law by implication says you are responsible for what you repel. How many times have you wanted something-perhaps a dream job or a meaningful relationship or a big opportunity-and didn't get it? How many times have you told yourself that the fault lay in circumstances, in the people around you, or just in "bad luck"? Then, the Law of Vibration makes us confront our demons: the fact that if we are vibrating in scarcity, negativity, or fear, we end up repelling those people and opportunities that could transform our lives.

## THOUGHTS AND EMOTIONS: THE TOOLS OF FREQUENCY

It's impossible to discuss the Law of Vibration without addressing the central role of thoughts and emotions. Thoughts generate a specific vibration, but emotions are even more powerful. Feeling something intensely is like sending a vibrational wave to the universe, reinforcing a particular frequency.

For example, thinking about success with enthusiasm or thinking about love with gratitude creates a high vibration that attracts compatible situations. But on the other hand, thoughts of doubt, envy, or resentment create a low frequency that often ends up attracting more experiences that reinforce those same feelings.

Science, in fact, is beginning to explore this invisible dimension. Quantum physics studies suggest that particles respond to the observer's observation and intention. Although there is still much to be unraveled, this invites us to reflect on the impact of our thoughts and feelings.

In some way, we are shaping reality around us with the frequencies we emit, and the Law of Vibration acts as the "bridge" between what we feel inside and what we live outside.

## THE CHALLENGE OF CHANGING YOUR INTERNAL FREQUENCY

But putting that all aside, lining up with the frequency of what you want isn't just about "thinking positively" or "faking happiness." It calls for an authenticity, a self-awareness that's rarely discussed. It means to confront and challenge beliefs and emotional patterns you've had for years, possibly even since childhood.

They are carved out of a lifetime of conditioning, family, cultural, and personal influences-our vibrational patterns do not just fall from the sky. In so doing, an individual should raise the frequency by releasing old energies that vibrate at a low frequency, and thus creating new patterns in design for what they truly desire.

Someone who desires prosperity yet lives their life filled with fear of lack is vibrating at a frequency that repels abundance. A person wanting to witness love yet holds onto resentment about past relationships continues to vibrate in frequencies of hurt and distrust. Transformation begins at that instant when you make up your mind to change-not only what you think but what you deeply feel-about each particular aspect of your life.

## THE CONSCIOUS PRACTICE OF RAISING VIBRATION

The Law of Vibration invites us to develop a conscious practice of raising frequency, and this begins with creating a daily "vibrational hygiene."

Ask yourself: How am I feeling right now? What am I thinking? Are these vibrations aligned with my dreams and goals? The practice can involve techniques such as meditation, visualization, and affirmations, but above all, it requires a stance of self-awareness and constant adjustment.

It's not something you do once. It's a gradual, dynamic process of "fine-tuning" with the reality you wish to create.

In the end, the Law of Vibration challenges you with a commitment: to accept that you are an active co-creator of your world. It invites you to see that the energy you emit is the raw material of your life and that, by adjusting your inner vibration, you adjust what you attract and experience.

This may be a difficult concept to accept, especially when life presents challenges. However, the beauty of this principle lies precisely in its powerful simplicity: change your vibration, and your reality will change.

# CHAPTER II:
## The Law of Cause and Effect

# YOU CHOOSE YOUR FUTURE

The Law of Cause and Effect, often called the "Law of Return," is one of the universe's most fundamental principles and, at the same time, one of the most powerful. It states that every action generates a reaction, and every decision we make, whether big or small, triggers inevitable consequences that shape our reality.

This law goes beyond a simple relationship between actions and results; it is a framework of accountability, inviting us to recognize that everything we put out into the world—whether in thought, emotion, or deed—returns to us in some form.

Those who understand the depth of this law know that nothing is truly "accidental" in their lives. They accept that the events they experience are natural responses to causes they themselves established, whether consciously or unconsciously. And this changes everything, as it places you in the role of creator, not victim. If every effect has a cause and every cause generates an effect, then every moment is an opportunity to plant seeds that will flourish in the future. This is the beauty (and challenge) of the Law of Cause and Effect.

## RESPONSIBILITY FOR OUR CHOICES

The Law of Cause and Effect seems to appeal to our need, as a human race, to apply blame on external circumstances for the happenings in life. How many times have we blamed our luck in life upon circumstances, fate, and even other people's actions? This law teaches us that, really and truly, we are the ones planting the seeds of our destiny. Even when we cannot choose what happens to us in the world, we are free to choose how to respond to that-and that response will itself be a cause capable of producing its own effects.

It doesn't mean you're "guilty" for everything that happens in your life, but it does mean that, starting from the moment you're aware of this truth, you have the ability to create consciously.

When you act with integrity, courage, and responsibility, then the result is positive and constructive. And when you act out of negligence, fear, or deception, then life will reflect those energies in your direction as difficult situations.

## THE SUBTLETY OF INTERNAL CAUSES

It's easy to think that the Law of Cause and Effect applies only to external actions, but that's a misconception. The most powerful causes are not always visible to others; they lie within our thoughts, beliefs, and intentions.

What you think, believe, and feel creates an energy field that attracts corresponding experiences. If you believe the world is a hostile place, you will inevitably attract situations that confirm this view. If, on the other hand, you believe in opportunity and abundance, your perception and actions will open doors to experiences that align with those beliefs.

Therefore, to change external effects, you must start by changing internal causes. Examine your beliefs, motivations, and intentions. Often, we act from hidden fears or an unconscious belief in limitation. When you begin to transform your internal causes, external effects inevitably begin to change.

## PLANTING CONSCIOUS SEEDS FOR THE FUTURE

The Law of Cause and Effect does give one pretty strong lesson: the present is literally the fertile ground upon which you plant seeds for your future. Every little decision plays an active part in the blueprint of one's reality.

You are now reaping the effects of the causes you planted yesterday, and tomorrow you will reap the results of what you plant today.

This concept is one that is so empowering, yet it presents its own set of challenges. It means that for a different future, one has to commit to new choices today. And if you want more prosperity, ask yourself: "What seeds of abundance can I plant now?" Want healthier relationships? Ask yourself: "Am I being the kind of person I want to attract? It's a process through which to harmonize your actions with your goals and to act in concert with those principles that are to govern your life.

## BREAKING THE CYCLE OF NEGATIVE CAUSES

Few people realize that they keep creating difficulties and frustrations through the same causes continually building up and thereby create the same effects.

The first step in this chain-reaction pattern is to become aware of the thought patterns, attitudes, and behavior which create such continuations of undesirable effects. Attempt to act with consciousness about the circumstances rather than automatic reactions; choose different causes for new results.

Every time one is faced with something challenging, it is decided again: to react just the same old way and create the same cause or to make a new cause which opens the way to a different effect.

This does indeed require a certain amount of self-awareness as well as some discipline, but the more you practice, the more it will become easy for you to replace those causes of destruction with constructive ones.

## THE POWER OF CONSCIOUSNESS IN THE CAUSE-EFFECT CYCLE

The Law of Cause and Effect is nothing to fear but to be mastered. It puts back in your hands the power of creation and teaches you through conscious action that the course of life may be steered.

Every conscious choice, every elevated thought, and every positive action ripples out into the universe, building a future that reflects your best self.

The Law of Cause and Effect empowers any person for a purpose-driven life and a life full of fulfillment. It truly helps one learn that, in fact, nothing is outside one's control when it comes to the causes one decides to plant and what intentions one wants to foster.

By living in harmony with this law, you understand that while you may not be in control of all events occurring around you, you can be in control of the quality of causes you create, knowing those causes are the seeds of a future full of endless possibilities.

# CHAPTER III:
## The Law of Attraction and Repulsion

# CLEAR INTENTION

One of the most interesting and, simultaneously, misunderstood universal laws is the Law of Attraction and Repulsion. It teaches that not only are we attracting what we want, but we are also repelling what we do not want, whether through conscious or unconscious means. This law is based upon the very principle that our thoughts, feelings, and actions emit a vibrational energy that interacts with the frequencies of the universe, thus attracting or repelling experiences that correspond with these energies.

While many people understand it merely as the ability to "attract" good things into our lives, the truth is that the Law of Attraction is not a one-dimensional ability. It rather involves attractions and repulsions of energies, people, situations, and even opportunities. Understanding this dynamic is important for us to apply this law more consciously and constructively.

**THE ATTRACTIVE ENERGY: THE POWER OF FREQUENCY**

The Law of Attraction is based upon the philosophy that "like attracts like"; that is, whatever you emit on an energetic level has the tendency to manifest within your reality.

When you align yourself with positive thoughts, uplifted feelings, and clear intentions, you will project a vibrational frequency that attracts circumstances and people which resonate with that energy. Joy brings about more joy, gratitude brings about things to be grateful for, and confidence brings about success opportunities.

But the key with the Law of Attraction, per se, is not to think positively but vibrate in concert with what you are trying to attract. In such a way, when one aligns deeply with the frequency of what one desires, the universe naturally reflects that as a response. The mind and heart must unite in the same energy for the vibrational field created to become strongly coherent enough to materialize what one desires.

## REPULSION: THE FORCE OF DISALIGNMENT

While attraction is often the focus when talking about the Law of Attraction, repulsion also plays a crucial role. Often, we are so focused on what we want to attract that we ignore the energies we are repelling – which can be just as powerful, if not more harmful.

Repulsion occurs when our beliefs, fears, and emotions are misaligned with our conscious intentions. When we have insecurities or thoughts of scarcity, for example, we are emitting a vibration of lack, which paradoxically ends up repelling what we want to attract. Instead of creating space for abundance, we create an invisible barrier that repels the opportunities and situations that could bring us prosperity.

Moreover, when we focus intensely on something we don't want, such as the fear of failure or anxiety about the future, we are also emitting a frequency that attracts exactly what we fear.

The very energy of resistance creates a repelling reaction, pushing away what we desire, because, in fact, we are energizing fear, doubt, and lack.

## THE IMPORTANCE OF EMOTIONAL ALIGNMENT

Actually, the Law of Attraction and Repulsion works with the use not just of thoughts but also of emotions. Emotions are that gasoline, which moves our vibrations and makes them more powerful or weaker. The point of using this law correctly is to align your emotions with your thoughts and intentions.

For instance, if one is focusing on abundance, one is not just to think of money but to write out a clear statement of exactly what that money goal is. You have to feel worthy of receiving abundance. Because if inside of your mind you are holding onto the conviction that money is scarce, or that you don't deserve success, then that turns into a repulsion-a pushing away of the very opportunity that would be available to bring what you want.

Aligning your emotions with your desires does not mean you are disconnected from or in denial about reality. It simply means you practice controlling your emotions while trusting, being joyful, and feeling grateful because your energy can be vibrational, aligning to allow what you really desire.

## THE IMPORTANCE OF DETACHMENT

One of the biggest traps in the Law of Attraction and Repulsion is over-attachment to results.

Each time we are completely consumed with a certain outcome, we actually manifest a frequency of need and lack, and that attracts our desires away from us. Detachment does not mean giving up on our dreams or not having goals, but rather releasing the pressure and anxiety of how and when it's going to happen.

True power arises in the understanding that the universe doesn't respond to hurry or desperation but to trust and surrender.

When you allow yourself to let go of control without abandoning your vision, you create a frequency of fluidity where things can manifest more easily and naturally. Detachment lets you attract what you want without the gravity of anxiety, allowing the flow of energy to occur more harmoniously.

## ATTRACTION AND REPULSION IN PERSONAL RELATIONSHIPS

Human relationships are one of the areas most affected by the Law of Attraction and Repulsion.

Often, we attract into our lives people who resonate with our deepest beliefs and vibrations. If you have a negative view of relationships, you may attract partners who confirm that view, while if you believe in the possibility of healthy, mutual love, you will attract experiences that reflect that belief.

Moreover, the Law of Attraction and Repulsion also manifests in the dynamics of how we relate to others. When we are in alignment with the energy of love and trust, we attract those same feelings in return.

But when we are in a state of distrust, fear, or resentment, we create a vibration that repels love and harmony.

The key to creating healthier relationships is first aligning internally with love and respect, and then external relationships will begin to reflect that energy.

## HOW TO MASTER THE LAW OF ATTRACTION AND REPULSION

True mastery over the Law of Attraction and Repulsion comes from self-awareness and control of one's energies. To master this law, you must learn to cultivate positive thoughts, aligned emotions, and clear intention, while also eliminating limiting beliefs, fears, and energies of resistance that may repel what you want.

The first step is always becoming conscious of your internal vibrations. Observe your thoughts and feelings. What are you attracting and repelling in your life right now? Identifying the thought and emotional patterns that are out of alignment with your desires is the first step in changing the affects you are creating.

With practice and patience, you can learn to use both attraction and repulsion consciously, aligning your energies with the results you wish to manifest. By mastering this law, you become the architect of your own reality, creating experiences that resonate with your deepest desires and beliefs.

# CHAPTER IV:
## The Law of Detachment

# LET LIFE FLOW

The Law of Detachment is one of the most profound and transformative principles for those seeking a life of peace, abundance, and alignment with the universe. It teaches us that to truly manifest our desires, we need to release the need to control the process and allow things to unfold naturally. In a culture that values control and obsesses over results, detachment may seem counterintuitive, but it is, in fact, an essential key to fulfillment.

## THE CONCEPT OF DETACHMENT

Detachment does not mean giving up on your dreams or abandoning your goals. Instead, it means releasing the anxiety and fear about the final outcome and trusting that the universe will bring what is best for you at the right time.

Detachment requires a balance between action and surrender, between persistence and the confidence that everything will unfold as it should. When we become obsessed with results, we emit a vibration of scarcity and need, which ends up repelling what we desire. On the other hand, when we are detached, we create an open and receptive energy field that attracts what we truly want.

## THE ROLE OF TRUST

Detachment is deeply connected with trust. Trusting the universe means believing that everything happens for a reason and that everything unfolds at the right time. To detach, it is necessary to develop an unshakable faith that even if things don't turn out exactly as planned, there is a higher intelligence working for your benefit.

This trust does not imply passivity or a lack of ambition but rather an openness to allow the natural process to happen.

When we trust the universe, we eliminate the burden of excessive control and fear, creating space for manifestation to occur more authentically and fluidly.

## DETACHMENT AND THE EGO

Detachment also involves recognizing and managing the ego. The ego is that part of us that desires security, control, and external validation, often leading us to a relentless pursuit of immediate success.

The ego craves visible results and guarantees that we're on the right path, but the universe operates on a deeper, more intuitive level. When we cling to the ego, we create resistance and limit our ability to attract what is truly beneficial for us.

Detachment, in many ways, is an act of humility. It means accepting that we do not know everything and that we don't have control over all aspects of our lives. This acknowledgment allows us to open up to possibilities the ego could never predict.

## THE PARADOX OF DESIRE AND DETACHMENT

Detachment does not mean eliminating desire. Desire is a creative force that drives our lives and motivates us to grow.

However, when we become excessively attached to our desires, we create pressure and emotional dependency that push us away from what we really want.

The true power of manifestation lies in balancing the intensity of desire with the willingness to release control over how and when the desire will be fulfilled.

When we genuinely desire something and then let go of that desire, we allow the universe to organize the ideal circumstances. This is the paradox of detachment: the more we let go, the easier it becomes to attract what we want. Detachment is not giving up; it is a deep trust in the universe's abundance.

## PRACTICES FOR CULTIVATING DETACHMENT

Cultivating detachment is a process that requires practice and patience. Here are some practices that can help develop this skill:

**Meditation and mindfulness:** Practicing mindfulness and meditation helps to calm the mind and reduce the desire for control. These practices allow you to connect with the present moment and trust the process more.

**Visualization without attachment:** Visualize your desires and dreams clearly, but then let go of that mental image and trust that the universe is working to bring it to fruition.

**Daily gratitude:** Practicing daily gratitude helps to reduce anxiety about the future and appreciate what you already have. Gratitude is a powerful form of detachment because it connects us with the abundance of the present moment.

**Acceptance of divine timing:** Accepting that everything happens at the right time is fundamental to detachment. When we learn to trust divine timing, our anxiety about the future decreases, and we begin to enjoy the journey.

## THE BENEFITS OF DETACHMENT

By mastering the Law of Detachment, you experience a range of benefits beyond simply manifesting desires.

Detachment brings deep inner peace, a sense of freedom, and a greater understanding of your role in the universe.

When we detach, we release the weight of expectations and become more receptive to new opportunities, relationships, and experiences.

Additionally, detachment increases our ability to respond to difficult situations with serenity, as we are no longer bound to a single outcome. With an open mind and a calm heart, we become agents of positive change in our own lives and in the lives of others.

## LIVING WITH DETACHMENT

Detachment is not a skill that develops overnight but rather a path that requires practice and commitment. However, when we truly embrace detachment, we discover a freedom that transcends our limited understanding of control. We begin to live more aligned with the laws of the universe, allowing our lives to flow naturally and with purpose.

Detachment is the ultimate act of trust in the universe. It is the surrender of our desires, fears, and expectations, with the certainty that we are being guided.

When we live with detachment, we become more open, confident, and at peace, knowing that we are exactly where we are meant to be and that everything will unfold at the right time.

# CHAPTER V:
## The Law of Inspired Action

# ACTION IS THE UNIVERSAL KEY

The Law of Inspired Action teaches us that to manifest our desires, we need to go beyond mere visualization or intention and take actions aligned with our goals.

While many people believe that the power of the mind alone is enough to attract what they want, inspired action emerges as an essential element to transform energy and intention into concrete results. The difference here is that the action is not merely a rational or planned response, but an intuitive response, flowing from an inner impulse that guides us on the right path.

## WHAT IS INSPIRED ACTION?

Inspired action is born from a place of alignment with your purpose and intuition. It's not about taking action just for the sake of it, nor does it rely on excessive effort or resistance. Instead, it's a type of action that feels natural, almost inevitable, as if you are being guided to make a particular decision or follow a specific path. It's when you feel compelled to do something, even if you don't fully understand the "why" at the moment.

This action is far more effective than a rigid plan or relentless effort.

When we follow the call of inspired action, we sync with the energies of the universe and position ourselves to attract the right opportunities and the right people into our lives.

## THE DIFFERENCE BETWEEN ACTION AND EXCESSIVE EFFORT

Inspired action is often confused with hard, persistent work. However, inspired action doesn't require the kind of effort that exhausts or drains you. On the contrary, it energizes you and brings a sense of lightness, as if the path is naturally unfolding.

While excessive effort is driven by fear of missing out or the need for control, inspired action is guided by trust and faith.

When we act from this place of trust, the universe responds favorably, removing obstacles and easing progress. This is the fundamental difference: effort creates resistance, while inspired action flows and aligns with the energy of our desire.

## HOW TO IDENTIFY INSPIRED ACTION

Recognizing inspired action requires a deep connection to your intuition and an inner silence to hear the universe's call. Here are some signs that you're facing inspired action:

**Strong intuition:** You feel an almost magnetic urge to do something or talk to someone. This urge comes effortlessly and brings with it a sense of urgency or purpose.

**Synchronicities:** Sometimes, inspired action presents itself through synchronicities. People, events, and opportunities seem to align in surprising ways, as if the universe is opening the right doors for you.

**Joy and enthusiasm:** When you feel joy and enthusiasm thinking about doing something, this may be a sign that it's inspired action. True inspired action brings a feeling of pleasure and alignment.

**Inner peace:** Even if the action seems risky or new, it brings a sense of inner peace and confidence, as if it's the natural next step.

## OPENING YOURSELF TO RECEIVE INSPIRATION

For inspired action to become part of your life, it's essential to create space for inspiration to arise. This means quieting the voices of doubt, fear, and worry, and allowing the silence of intuition to take their place. Some practices that can help with this process include:

**Meditation:** Meditation is one of the best ways to calm the mind and listen to your inner voice. By practicing meditation, you create a receptive space where inspiration can flow freely.

**Intuition journal:** Writing down your thoughts, ideas, and impulses can help you identify patterns and moments of inspiration. Revisiting these entries can reveal important insights about your next step.

**Trust in the process:** Often, inspiration arises subtly and without apparent logic. Trusting the process and what your intuition tells you is crucial to acting in alignment.

## THE BENEFITS OF INSPIRED ACTION

Acting in line with inspiration has many benefits. When we follow these "nudges" from the universe, we often encounter less resistance, and more opportunities come our way.

This kind of action keeps us in a state of flow, where obstacles seem smaller and progress becomes faster and easier.

Inspired action also brings a sense of purpose and fulfillment. Each step taken on this journey feels like part of a larger plan, and this sense of personal meaning and alignment can transform even the simplest tasks into something deeply rewarding.

## TRUST AND FOLLOW THE CALL

The Law of Inspired Action reminds us that manifesting our desires is not passive.

It requires the courage to listen to and follow our instincts and intuitions, even when the path isn't entirely clear. Each act of trust strengthens our connection with the universe and brings us closer to our dreams.

So, trust your intuition and act from that place of inner certainty. Allow the universe to guide your steps, knowing that each inspired action brings you closer to realizing your deepest desires. The universe is ready to collaborate with you — you just need to be open and receptive to listen and follow the call.

# CHAPTER VI:
## The Law of Persistence and Faith

# NEVER GIVE UP

The Law of Persistence and Faith plays an elemental role in the journey of manifestation. As much as it's key to have your thoughts, intentions, and actions aligned to what it is that you want, persistence and undaunted faith serve to add fuel to those desires.

This law teaches us that at any path, hindrances are inevitable; the only way to true success is going with the tide or through it, trusting in our bones deeper that what we want is doable and within reach.

## THE POWER OF PERSISTENCE

It doesn't mean doggedly continuing in set patterns, but instead refusing to allow what might be temporary setbacks to become permanent roadblocks. In the manifestation process, persistence means always realigning oneself with one's goals, keeping the vision alive and committed to your way even when results are not immediately apparent.

True persistence comes from a place of inner resilience and commitment, knowing that each and every step, regardless of their size, is taking you closer to your dreams.

Persistence also means embracing challenges as part of the process. So often, the universe gives us tests to solidify our desires, refine our intentions, and prove our commitments.

These can be really, really uncomfortable, but these remind us that sometimes it is not always easy along the way in manifesting. It is in persistence that one finds determination that hardens with time, and this resolve, finally unbreakable, is what enables them to reach their goals.

## THE ROLE OF FAITH

Faith is knowing, undaunted, that what one desires is possible, even when the outer circumstances absolutely deny this fact. It is a question of trusting in the unseen and believing in outcomes which as yet are not visible.

Faith is a powerful ally in manifestation because it bridges the gap between where you are now and where you want to be.

Faith requires us to believe in the timing of the universe, which usually does not align with our expectations. The path leading to our dreams might be filled with detours or delays, and it is at those moments that faith is tested. In such instances of doubt or frustration, faith simply involves believing that the universe has a plan and that each experience serves a purpose-even if not immediately apparent.

Faith is also a sort of anchor that keeps us aligned and steady with our intentions. When doubts arise, as they invariably do, it is faith that gives us the courage to forge ahead, knowing that all our efforts are not in vain.

## COMBINING PERSISTENCE AND FAITH

Persistence and faith are complementary forces. Without faith, persistence may burn out or frustrate since at times it is a fight against the tide. Similarly, faith without persistence turns into a passive attitude, since one is merely hoping without trying to act.

Merging these two forces together brings a dynamic momentum, which moves us toward our goals, determined and confident.

Those who understand the law of behavior know that every step taken, no matter how minute, is an affirmation to the self of one's faith in the vision. In that act of persistence through challenges, these people remain loyal to faith in things unseen and thereby achieve rock-solid energetic alignment between themselves and their desires. This alignment attracts desires into reality, sometimes in unimaginable and extraordinary ways.

## PATIENCE IN EMBRACING THE JOURNEY

Manifestation is all about faith in the outcome, but one must also have faith in the process. Patience can be one version of faith in action; it's the ability to wait without losing hope or giving in to impatience. Whenever we hurry or force any outcome, it disrupts the natural flow of energy and creates resistance. Allowing ourselves to embrace the journey with patience signals to the universe that we trust in its timing.

Patience can also enable us to remain open to possibilities and direction that might come our way. Most times, the universe envisages something bigger for our lives than what we can actually perceive, and through patience, we leave ourselves open to results that might even be better than what we initially intended.

## OVERCOMING DOUBT AND RESISTANCE

One of the major hindrances to manifestation involves doubt. It is natural sometimes to experience moments of doubt, especially whenever things are not working out as they should.

We must learn, however, that this can usually be rooted in fear, or an aspect of the mind seeking control.

Consciously, we can decide to focus on faith instead of doubt and hence view setbacks as opportunities rather than failures.

Persistence with faith works as a huge antidote to doubt. Each time we persist in the face of doubt, renewing our faith with every setback, we send a loud and clear message to the universe that our desires are unwavering. In such a way, unshakable belief acts like a magnet to attract into life all the circumstances, people, and opportunities necessary to bring our desires into being.

## THE REWARDS OF PERSISTENCE AND FAITH

Yet, the rewards of embracing the Law of Persistence and Faith go much deeper than simply goal realization. The Law actually manages to turn lives around, for it molds and shapes within us qualities like resilience, inner strength, and a deep sense of purpose.

Once a commitment has been made to a given path, this law tends to render one's life more assured and empowered, in which case the light at the end of the tunnel-qua surmounting of every kind of obstacles in life-is guaranteed.

Then persistence and faith create a lasting alignment with the energy of abundance. Those working with this law not only fulfill their desires but very often exceed them, realizing that the journey itself is the reward, the person they become in the course of that journey.

# CHAPTER VII:
## The Law of Balance and Harmony

# BALANCE EVERYTHING

The Law of Balance and Harmony teaches us that true fulfillment comes from maintaining inner harmony and a balanced approach to all areas of life. In the journey of manifestation, it's essential not only to focus on desires and goals but also to ensure that our energy flows healthily and consistently.

Without balance, even the most powerful intentions can become unsustainable. When our lives are in harmony, we create a foundation that allows for continuous growth, well-being, and the manifestation of our highest potential.

## THE IMPORTANCE OF INNER HARMONY

Inner harmony is the state of being at peace with oneself. It is achieved when our thoughts, emotions, and actions are aligned with our values and purpose.

When we are in a state of inner harmony, we become more receptive to the energies around us, which allows for clearer guidance, stronger intuition, and a greater sense of contentment. Inner harmony helps us stay resilient in the face of challenges, as it provides a calm center from which we can navigate life's fluctuations.

This inner peace also creates a positive energy field that influences our relationships, our work, and our ability to manifest our desires. When we are internally balanced, we become less reactive and more intentional, enabling us to make choices that align with our true selves.

## BALANCING LIFE'S AREAS

Balance involves paying attention to the various aspects of our lives: career, relationships, health, personal growth, and spiritual practice. Neglecting one area often creates imbalances that can hinder our overall well-being. For example, an intense focus on career might lead to burnout, while ignoring personal relationships can result in loneliness and isolation.

To cultivate balance, it's essential to regularly assess each area of life and make conscious adjustments as needed. The goal is not to achieve perfection in every area but to foster a sense of wholeness where all aspects support each other.

A balanced life brings a sense of stability, allowing our energy to circulate freely and creating a fertile ground for manifestation.

## PRACTICES FOR CULTIVATING PEACE AND INTERNAL ALIGNMENT

Maintaining balance and harmony requires intentional practices that nurture both the body and mind. Here are some suggestions to help you cultivate peace and alignment within yourself:

**Mindfulness meditation:** Practicing mindfulness helps us stay present, reduces stress, and strengthens our connection to our inner self. Through meditation, we develop awareness of our thoughts and emotions, which allows us to respond more intentionally to life's situations.

**Energy clearing:** Engaging in practices like breathwork, yoga, or energy healing can help release blockages and allow energy to flow freely. These practices create an internal balance that enhances both physical and emotional health.

**Setting healthy boundaries:** Balance requires that we set limits with ourselves and others. Learning to say "no" to activities or relationships that drain us is a crucial part of maintaining harmony.

**Self-care:** Taking care of your body through exercise, nutrition, and rest is essential for maintaining balance. Self-care is not selfish; it is necessary to ensure that you have the energy to pursue your goals and engage meaningfully with others.

**Journaling:** Reflecting on your thoughts and emotions through journaling helps bring awareness to areas where you might be feeling unbalanced. Writing regularly can reveal patterns and insights that allow you to make conscious adjustments.

## EMBRACING IMPERFECTION

The pursuit of balance and harmony does not mean striving for a flawless life. Life is inherently dynamic, and balance is a fluid state that changes over time. Embracing imperfection allows us to move flexibly with life's ups and downs without feeling overwhelmed or defeated. Balance is a journey, not a destination, and it's okay to recalibrate along the way.

By allowing ourselves to be imperfect, we become more compassionate toward ourselves and others. This self-compassion reinforces inner peace and helps us remain centered, regardless of external circumstances.

## THE BENEFITS OF A BALANCED LIFE

A balanced life creates an environment where manifestation becomes more natural and sustainable. When we cultivate harmony and balance, we are better able to maintain focus, handle challenges, and sustain the positive energy required for manifestation. Inner harmony makes us more resilient, helping us to recover from setbacks more quickly and stay aligned with our vision.

Additionally, a balanced approach to life allows us to enjoy the journey. Manifestation is not solely about reaching a goal but also about experiencing joy and fulfillment along the way. By maintaining balance, we create space for moments of happiness, connection, and gratitude that enrich our lives.

# CHAPTER VIII:
## Play the Game Consciously

# CELEBRATE LIFE

The notion of life as a game gives us a new perspective on the way we can think about our goals, challenges, and relationships. In this chapter, we look in more detail at how to consciously play the game, that is, through making choices which serve our intentions and values.

When we realize that life plays according to specific universal rules, we may be more aware of the choices that we make and the consequence of those choices in relationship to our journey. It means taking responsibility for our reality, being conscious of our role as creators, and living with purposefulness, clarity, and integrity.

## CONSCIOUSNESS: A FIRST STEP TOWARD CONSCIOUS LIVING

Awareness is, in fact, the very foundation of a conscious life: learning how the game will be played and especially the way our thoughts, emotions, and actions mold our experiences. This awareness involves not only action but also the inner observation-observing our patterns of mind, our responses to emotions, and underlying motives.

In this objective observation of the self, we can gauge which parts of our lives need improvement, thus taking measures to correct ourselves to live the reality we want to be experiencing.

Awareness is also presence. The more we are in the now, the easier it will be to respond to challenges and opportunities presented by life. We are intuitive, creative, and insightful when we have awareness. In that respect, we can live through our intuition and make conscious choices that further our growth.

## THE POWER OF INTENTION

Intention is the compass of this game called life. The moment one begins to set a clear intention, directionality and a sense of purpose immediately come with it.

When there is no intention, one only goes along and waits for things to happen-when, in fact, life is asking you to direct the circumstances instead of just being at their mercy. Playing consciously means definition of what one wants and why he wants it, followed by every action oriented to go in that direction.

These intentions can be as broad or specific as we will decide, but what is most important is to make them authentic and come from the deepest values. When our intentions are clear, then the universe responds by aligning circumstances and opportunities to help us in the attainment of our goals. But conscious intention does call for a commitment to self-honesty because oftentimes one has to let go of the ego-driven desires and focus on what truly fulfills us.

## ACCOUNTABILITY FOR OUR CHOICES

The first aspect of playing consciously involves taking full responsibility for our lives. Shifting the blame to the people around us, or even to events beyond their control, is so convenient, but this inhibits growth and keeps us in our passive role. In this regard, taking responsibility means recognizing that while we may not have a choice sometimes over what happens to us, we certainly can control the response we make and what actions we take against it.

By taking responsibility, we take back our power as creators. In turn, this allows us to grow and change our lives at will. To take responsibility does not mean to accept guilt or blame; it means to be empowered, free. We may allow a sense of agency through ownership of our actions that enables us to mold and shape our future in a particular direction.

## CHANGE AND UNCERTAINTY

In the game of life, change is the only constant. The aware player is never in rebellion against the fact but learns to live with this prospect. Change evidences growth, new experiences, and learning processes. Upon acceptance of the inevitability of change, resilience and adaptability-two most important qualities for overcoming ups and downs-become part of our psychic makeup. Uncertainty can be daunting, yet it also ushers in new possibilities. Instead of responding to uncertainty with fear, we approach times of uncertainty with curiosity, and that makes us much more susceptible to unexpected opportunities and insights. The conscious player of the game of life learns to flow with change, trusting that each twist and turn has a purpose-even if immediately unclear.

## CULTIVATING A MINDSET OF GROWTH AND LEARNING

Conscious living requires a growth mindset. A growth mindset embraces failures as necessary and valuable learning experiences, not final. Every mistake or setback prepares us for developing insights into how we could do better, be different, and live our lives with a twist in time to come.

With continuous learning, we keep our spirits high, even amidst difficulties, and remain open toward growth in every area of our life.

Aware players also know that growth is a lifelong game. They read voraciously, stay curious, and are unafraid to let go of assumptions when proved wrong. It keeps us engaged, adaptable, and ready for whatever comes next in life.

## LIVING WITH INTEGRITY AND ALIGNMENT

Integrity presupposes coherence among values, intentions, and actions. Consciously playing this game, we must live in a coherent and true manner according to our premises.

If we live with integrity, we generate coherence inside and engender trust in people. This integrity connects us more strongly with the universe since we act from the place of truthfulness, sincerity, and intention.

Living in alignment means making choices that are representative of who we truly are: setting boundaries, speaking our truth, and staying congruent with our principles.

This is the powerful energetic alignment that occurs when our actions are in alignment with our intention, which in turn supports the manifestation process and allows us to live with confidence and peace.

## CELEBRATE THE JOURNEY

The game of life is not about winning; it is about living meaningfully. To play consciously means to know the journey well as much as the destination.

Every moment, every lesson, and every experience brought us to who we're becoming. Joy and gratitude in the journey create a full life of purpose and connection.

Celebrating the journey means acknowledging our progress, however small. Every step forward, each obstacle overcome, and every insight gained counts and is worthy of being acknowledged. In appreciation of the journey lies a positive feedback spiral that energizes us and further reinforces our commitment to conscious living.

## MAKING UP YOUR OWN RULES

The game of life is unique to the individual. Though there be universal laws governing all, specific goals, values, and desires are deeply personal. Playing consciously means taking the freedom to create your own "rules"-standards mirroring your unique values, passions, and vision that help guide you toward what really matters in the creation of a true and fulfilling life.

By creating your rules, you are releasing yourself from the shackles of what society has imposed on you, setting yourself free to live by standards that you set for yourself. It's a deeply self-defining act-powerful in its assertion of autonomy and self-respect, reinforcing one's position as a conscious creator of their reality.

# CHAPTER IX:
Case Studies

# PUTTING IT INTO PRACTICE

## CASE STUDY:
## How Carlos Went from Financial Struggle to Business Success

Growing up in a small town in Brazil, Carlos Mendes had always been extremely enthusiastic about design. As a child, he had an ambitious dream - his own interior design firm, turning spaces into works of art reflecting functionality with beauty. But this dream hardly materialized smoothly. Soon after graduation, Carlos made it a point to relocate to São Paulo, the frenetic hub of Brazil's design industry. The city, all tarred and glued together and running on perhaps the most vibrant of cultures, was the perfect world for him to start his career. But soon enough, he found himself face to face with bitter realities. All he could find for years were low-paid jobs, which barely allowed him to pay his rent and other basic living expenses. He had been in an endless debt cycle, and his dream of trying to establish his own business was now a far-off call.

It was while in this state of utter despair and confusion that the idea first came to him that life is a game with laws that can be applied to it. Curious yet skeptical, he began reading literature on these principles, primarily the Law of Vibration, the Law of Cause and Effect, and the Law of Attraction and Repulsion. Although he was very skeptical at first, the place to which life had brought him urged him to embrace those ideas in the hope they would show a way out of his endless troubles.

First, Carlos applied what he'd learned about the Law of Vibration: every thought and emotion has a vibration that attracts an experience. With a constant stream of feelings of worry and lack regarding money, he was keeping his vibration low-one in which opportunity couldn't locate him. To reverse this, Carlos began a daily gratitude practice. Every day he would list five things he was grateful for: his health, good friends, his abiding passion for designing, and minor successes that happened on the job site. It was a little thing-simple-but it did the trick. As his attitude changed, the little things in his life started changing. His interactions at work became more positive, his levels of stress went down, and he began to feel optimistic once again. This emotional shift created an openness in him that he hadn't felt in years, which allowed him to think more clearly and strategically about his goals.

With a more positive mind, Carlos turned his attention to the Law of Cause and Effect. He knew then that every action taken, every choice made, was going to either bring him closer to that dream or farther away from it. Carlos had lived by this rule ever since he decided not to just sit around waiting for a break but to take matters into his own hands and begin to make investments in his future business. He started freelancing on weekends, taking on any low-level design work from friends and small businesses. In addition, he would attend networking events to meet potential clients and other partners. Not to say it involved working at God-awful times and juggling a number of jobs at once, but with this portfolio addition-in their own small way, adding up, building a little reputation in the highly competitive São Paulo design scene-gradually, Carlos felt more purposeful.

As the commercial attempts started to heat up, Carlos focused on the Law of Attraction and Repulsion. He knew he had to clarify his intentions first and truly believe that he could attract his ideal clients. Carlos gave a clear vision to his future business: he pictured in great detail the type of clients he wanted to attract and the kinds of high-value design projects he wanted to take on. He started doing daily affirmations, such as repeating to himself, "I'm a successful designer, and I attract clients who appreciate my vision and work." It became an affirmative focus that now began to show real results. Carlos went to a networking event and met a successful entrepreneur who was impressed enough with his passion and commitment to the work that he decided to offer him the opportunity to design a new café. The Carlos project turned out to be his breakthrough-a high-profile job that gave him a significant amount of exposure and somewhat vindicated his self-worth as a designer.

Not all months have been great monetarily, and there have been periods of uncertainty and self-doubt about whether he made the right decision to pursue his own business full-time. It was during these times that Carlos turned to the Law of Detachment, a fundamental that professes letting go of any need for attachment to the outcome, trusting that the universe has ways of bringing out the best at its own timing. Instead of the necessity of obsessing about every client and project, he could be taught to let go of his anxiety about the future. He focused on delivering his best work, regardless of immediate results, and trusted that the right opportunities would come in due time. In coming to this place, he felt his peace deepen, and his creative energy really flowered. As he let go of his fears and expectations, his clients started referring him to other prospects, and soon his workload grew steadily and organically.

As his business picked up pace, Carlos started to apply the Law of Inspired Action fully: to move intuitively and in alignment toward one's goals. He learned to follow intuition regarding which projects he should be working on and even which clients to take on-or not. He found this intuitive approach challenging yet empowering at the same time, since intuitive action allowed him to stay focused on those who valued his style and creativity. One day, he received a call from a luxury hotel chain looking for a designer to refurbish many suites. Though he had never done big hotel designs before, something from within urged him to take on this challenge. It became one of the most dramatic successes and showcased his skills on a higher level, culminating in media exposure. As Carlos's reputation soared, high-profile clients came running for his bold and innovative designs.

Carlos lived the Law of Persistence and Faith throughout his journey. The road to success was really rocky; there were many challenging clients, and sometimes the finances were strained. But he stuck with it, reminding himself daily of the vision and purpose that were important in the long run. Each challenge was an opportunity for growth, and setbacks never made him disheartened; rather, he learned from them. Apart from persistence, faith in himself and the Universe's plan made him take each step with determination and confidence. Each act of persistence reinforced his bond to the things he wanted to achieve, and faith in the unseen kept him in line with his vision when the path was not in sight.

Another important side of the road to success for Carlos was balancing his professional ambitions with personal well-being, guided by the Law of Balance and Harmony. He worked at keeping in harmony all areas of his life so that his energy flowed healthily and continuously. Carlos would also invest much in personal care, trying to find some time for family, friends, and self-improvement in the midst of the emerging business. Mindfulness meditation, exercise, and journaling helped him to connect with his core and be centered, thus nurturing this inner peace that started to spill over into his work and personal relationships.

Today, Carlos Mendes runs a successful interior design business with an enthusiastic team of designers who share his vision and values. He has transformed from a struggling designer hardly able to make ends meet into a successful entrepreneur with a reputation for excellence and creativity. That is a real testimony to how life changes when one applies the universal laws in living. As he aligned thoughts, emotions, and actions within these guiding principles, Carlos was able to go through financial struggles, build a successful business, and create a balanced and fulfilling life.

Carlos's story is a perfect example that success is not just a hand-woven outcome of effort or luck but an eclectic blend of intention, persistence, faith, and conscious alignment with universal laws. His transformation really proves that all people can realize their dreams through the conscious playing of the game of life and embracing each law as a guide to navigate both challenges and triumphs. With his commitment to and belief in these principles, Carlos found that the dream of owning a successful business fulfilled him on a much higher level of purpose and balance than he could have ever imagined and inspired others to embark on their journeys of living consciously and manifesting.

## CASE STUDY:
## Jessica's Quest from Pain to Healthy Relationships and Personal Fulfillment

Jessica Turner was born in small-town America, where she had learned since the first steps in her life how to find love everywhere. Yet, it was her early romantic experiences that first channeled her through a path full of hurt and insecurities. She had to face constant disappointments in her teenage relationship and grew to believe that true love demanded great sacrifices-sacrifices that for her included losing her identity and embracing abusive behaviors. This warped view of love was carried into adulthood as Jessica entered into relationships where the partners emotionally sucked her dry.

As an adult, Jessica entered a vicious circle of self-destruction with relationships. Her self-esteem was already poor, stemming from her childhood, but worsened even further since she constantly felt belittled and manipulated. She'd already been married twice before, both marriages resulting in painful breakups that continued to nurture those feelings that maybe she'll never find someone who will love her properly and healthily. At age 34 years old, Jessica was emotionally wrung out. Her friends started to fall away, and she lost all confidence in herself and her ability to create a healthy relationship. She felt she would never be able to break the cycle of suffering that seemed to be the norm in her love life.

It was then that Jessica began to study the universal laws after hearing about the transformative power of the Law of Attraction. The first law that she applied was that of vibration. Having long been skeptical, she felt she had nothing left to lose and opened herself up to new possibilities. Jessica started reading books about the power of the mind, attraction of positive energy, and invisible laws that governed people's lives. As she began to understand that her internal frequency was vibrating at a point associated with suffering and disappointment, she realized she needed to change the way she viewed and felt about herself. She began the daily practice of gratitude, which was hard at first to imagine, given the state of despair in which she found herself. She wrote in her journal every morning: "I am grateful for my health, my strong body, and my ability to learn and grow." Although these thoughts at first sounded hollow, after some time, Jessica started to feel light, as she hadn't in years.

By bringing her thoughts into alignment with positive frequency, Jessica found herself drawing more positivity into her life from people. Her energy began to shift, and she became more conscious of the choices she made as she slowly separated from abusive and toxic relationships that she otherwise would have repressed as normal. She realized that throughout the years, she had chosen abusive and toxic partners because she had low self-esteem, merely believing that love had to be earned at all costs, no matter how humiliating or degrading. Through the use of the Law of Attraction, Jessica started changing her expectations of relationships. She started focusing on building a vision of a partner that would respect her-loving, kind, and sharing values. She threw herself into attracting someone who appreciated her for what she truly was.

She also applied the Law of Cause and Effect, realizing that everything she had done so far, whether big or small, added up to her reality. Since she knew that calling into her life a healthy partnership would actually mean having to build a healthy relationship with herself, Jessica started making choices with a spotlight on self-care. She started going to therapy, meditating, working out, and paying attention to her nutrition. In the place of each small step, she felt her confidence grow. Not to mention that with this internal transformation, Jessica finally realized she was no longer attracting the wrong types of partners. Instead, she started meeting men who showed respect and consideration but still felt that there was something missing. She knew that although she was on a better path, she needed to align her desires even more with the universal laws.

It was then that Jessica decided to focus more intensely on the Law of Attraction and Repulsion. She realized that what she emitted into the world was indeed what she attracted into her world, and she worked at being her most authentic self consciously. No longer would she accept any relationship, no matter how good that relationship may seem. She raised the standards for the people she dealt with, knowing she deserved someone who could rise to her level in building something solid that would last. It was under this mindset that she met Mark.

Mark was another breed of man altogether from the men Jessica had met. He was in step with the positive energy cultivated in her life, sharing the same interests and values as herself. Most important of all, he treated her with respect. Unlike the men who had crossed her path previously, Mark respected her needs and dreams. Their relationship wasn't based on sacrifices or manipulations but on partnership, mutual trust, and joint growth. Another important role in their relationship was also played by the Law of Detachment. She finally got the message that, yes, she has to let go and trust the process since it is not forced; true love will naturally flow in. She is no longer afraid of being alone; instead, she trusts that when the time is right, her partner will come.

Not only did Jessica find true love, but she also learned to detach from this need for a relationship so as to be happy. She knew this meant trusting herself and allowing the universe to bring her what was best for her, rather than being in a relationship. She directed her attention to taking care of herself and to being the best partner she could be. This detachment from the expectation of needing a relationship was important. Mark and Jessica grew together into new adventures and goals. It was for this reason that they started an interior design business, something which they both loved, and with the laws of abundance and inspired action, it only prospered.

Their successful relationship also needed to employ the use of the Law of Persistence and Faith. Obviously like all other couples they passed through hell but they always had faith in themselves to overcome any obstacle. It is faith in love and to mutual commitment that cemented their relationship. They have then applied the Law of Balance and Harmony to their daily life, striving to balance work with their relationship, including self-care. They allowed time for family and friends and made time for one another so that their energies were always replenished and in vibration with the values they hold dear.

Jessica and Mark are married today and have two children. They built a business that was supporting them financially, yet at the same time feeding their passions and values. Jessica's journey proves that applying universal laws can really transform one's life-not only to find love but for true fulfillment and prosperity. Her story here shows that by aligning thoughts, feelings, and actions to the principles of universal laws, anyone can come out from the struggles of the past and create a future full of love, abundance, and happiness.

# YOU'RE VERY WELCOME FOR READING